KT-552-125

The Silly Little Book

of

STUPID

JOKES

The Silly Little Book
of

STUPID

JOKES

mustard

This edition published and distributed by Mustard, 1999

Mustard is an imprint of Parragon

Parragon
Queen Street House
4–5 Queen Street
Bath BA1 1HE

Produced by Magpie Books, an imprint of
Robinson Publishing Ltd, London

Copyright © Parragon 1999

All rights reserved. This book is sold subject to the condition
that it shall not, by way of trade or otherwise, be lent, re-sold, hired
out or otherwise circulated in any form of binding or cover other than
that in which it is published and without a similar condition including
this condition being imposed on the subsequent purchaser.

ISBN 0 75253 009 7

A copy of the British Library Cataloguing-in-Publication Data
is available from the British Library

Printed and bound in Singapore

Contents

Introduction

What kind of person thinks his bath is electric because it has a plug? An idiot, that's who. And as you will learn from these pages there are an awful lot of them about doing some pretty stupid things. But just beware; word tricks and limericks can make you or a friend look a bit of a fool too.

Word Play

Flash Harry gave his girlfriend a mink stole for her birthday. Well, it may not have been mink, but it's fairly certain it was stole.

Did you hear about the florist who had two children?
One's a budding genius and the other's a blooming idiot.

Why is classroom like an old car?
Because it's full of nuts, and has a
crank at the front.

Where can you dance in
California?
San Fran-disco.

What did the children do when
there were rock cakes for lunch?
Took their pick.

1st Undertaker: I've just been given the sack.
2nd Undertaker: Why?
1st Undertaker: I buried someone in the wrong place.
2nd Undertaker: That was a grave mistake.

What should you give short elves?
Elf-raising flour.

How do we know that Rome was built at night?
Because all the books say it wasn't built in a day!

Ben's dad was building a pine bookcase, and Ben was watching and occasionally helping. "What are the holes for?" Ben asked. "They're knot holes," said his dad. "What are they, then, if they're not holes?" said Ben.

Why do barbers make good drivers?
Because they know all the short cuts.

What's the difference between a square peg in a round hole and a kilo of lard?
One's a fat lot of good and the other's a good lot of fat!

What happens when business is
slow at a medicine factory?
You can hear a cough drop.

What do you get if you cross a
witch with an ice cube?
A cold spell.

Which two letters are rotten for
your teeth?
D K.

What did the "just married"
spiders call their new home?
Newlywebs.

Sign on the school noticeboard:
Guitar for sale, cheap, no strings
attached.

Darren, at school dinner: I've just
swallowed a bone.
Teacher: Are you choking?
Darren: No, I'm serious.

Girl: Shall I put the kettle on?
Boy: No, I think you look all right in the dress you're wearing.

What do you get if you cross a caretaker with a monk who smokes large cigars?
A caretaker with a bad habit.

Who carries a sack and bites people?
Santa Jaws

Sign outside the school caretaker's hut: Will the person who took my ladder please return it, or further steps will be taken.

When George left school he was going to be a printer. All the teachers said he was the right type.

What's the difference between an iced lolly and the school bully? You lick one, the others lick you.

Teacher to Dinner Lady: A pork chop, please and make it lean. Dinner Lady: Certainly, Mr Smith, which way?

Why did the man go out and buy a set of tools?
Because everyone kept telling him he had a screw loose.

What's the difference between a nail and a boxer?
One gets knocked in, the other gets knocked out.

A pilot flying over the jungle was having trouble with his plane and decided to bail out before it crashed. So he got into his parachute, jumped, pulled the rip-cord, and drifted gently down to land. Unfortunately he landed right in a large cooking pot which a tribal chief was simmering gently over a fire. The chief looked at him, rubbed his eyes, looked again, and asked, "What's this flier doing in my soup?"

Two fleas were sitting on Robinson
Crusoe's back as he lay on the
beach in the sun. "Well, so long,"
said one to the other, "I'll see you
on Friday."

Two fishermen were out in their
boat one day when a hand
appeared in the ocean.
"What's that?" asked the first
fisherman. "It looks as if
someone's drowning!"
"Nonsense," said the second. "It
was just a little wave."

What kind of bandage do people wear after heart surgery?
Ticker tape.

Did you hear about Mrs Dimwit's new baby? She thought babies should be pink, so she took this one to the doctor because it was a horrible yeller.

What happened to Ray when a
ten-ton truck ran over him?
He became X-Ray.

Did you hear about the boy who
got worried when his nose grew to
eleven inches long?
He thought it might turn into a
foot.

What do you do if you split your
sides laughing?
Run until you get a stitch.

Do undertakers enjoy their job?
Of corpse they do.

Teacher: Didn't you know the bell
had gone?
Silly Sue: I didn't take it, Miss.

Hil: Who was the fastest runner in history?
Bill: Adam. He was first in the human race.

Did you hear about the teacher who was trying to instil good table manners in her girls? She told them, "A well-brought-up girl never crumbles her bread or rolls in her soup."

Did you hear about the boy who was told to do 100 lines? He drew 100 cats on the paper. He thought the teacher had said "lions."

What's your handicrafts teacher like?
She's a sew and sew.

What gets bigger the more you take away?
A hole.

Why did the undertaker chop all
his corpses into little bits?
Because he liked them to rest in
pieces.

Why was the insect thrown out of
the forest?
Because he was a litter bug.

What did the undertaker say to his
girlfriend?
Em-balmy about you.

What happened when the pussy
swallowed a penny?
There was money in the kitty.

A young lad was helping his dad
with do-it-yourself jobs around
the house. "You know, son," said
the father, "you're just like
lightning with that hammer."
"Fast, eh?" said the boy.
"Oh, no – you never strike in the
same place twice."

What did the traffic light say to the motorist?
Don't look now, I'm changing.

What's the difference between a Peeping Tom and someone who's just got out of the bath?
One is rude and nosey. The other is nude and rosey.

Why did the lazy idiot apply for a job in a bakery?
He fancied a long loaf.

What's the difference between a sigh, a car and a monkey?
A sigh is oh dear. A car is too dear. A monkey is you, dear.

Was the carpenter's son a chip off the old block?

Do you serve women in this bar?
No sir, you have to bring your own.

What happens if you play table-
tennis with a bad egg?
First it goes ping, then it goes
pong.

Who is Wyatt Burp?
The sheriff with the repeater.

Why are school cooks cruel?
Because they batter fish and beat
eggs.

What's a giant's favorite tale?
A tall story.

My sister thinks that a juggernaut
is an empty beer mug.

What did the Eskimo children sing
when their principal was leaving?
Freeze a Jolly Good Fellow.

Ben's teacher regards Ben as a
wonder child. He wonders whether
he'll ever learn anything.

What do you get if you cross a
burglar with a concrete mixer?
A hardened criminal.

What's the difference between a crossword expert, a greedy boy and a pot of glue?
A crossword expert is a good puzzler and the greedy boy's a pud guzzler. The pot of glue? Ah, that's where you get stuck.

What's the difference between a kangaroo, a lumberjack and a bag of peanuts?

A kangaroo hops and chews and a lumberjack chops and hews.

Yes, but what's the bag of peanuts for?

For monkeys like you.

Who makes suits and eats spinach?

Popeye the Tailorman.

Where does Tarzan buy his
clothes?
At a Jungle Sale.

What kind of cans are there in
Mexico?
Mexicans.

What is a mermaid?
A deep-she fish.

Is this a second-hand shop?
Yes, sir.
Good. Can you fit one on my
watch, please?

In the park this morning I was
surrounded by lions.
Lions! In the park?
Yes – dandelions!

Notice (in a new shop window):
Don't go elsewhere and be robbed
– try us!

Jennifer: Are you coming to my party?
Sandra: No, I ain't going.
Jennifer: Now, you know what Miss told us. Not ain't. It's I am not going, he is not going, she is not going, they are not going.
Sandra: Blimey, ain't nobody going?

A noise woke me up this morning.
What was that?
The crack of dawn.

They're not going to grow bananas
any longer.
Really? Why not?
Because they're long enough
already.

I wonder where I got that puncture?
Maybe it was at that last fork in the road . . .

I bet I can make you speak like a Red Indian.
How?
That's right!

Passer-by (to fisherman): Is this river any good for fish?
Fisherman: It must be. I can't get any of them to leave it.

Why is perfume obedient?
Because it is scent wherever it goes.

Which soldiers smell of salt and pepper?
Seasoned troopers.

A man with a newt on his shoulder
walked into a pub. "What do you
call him?" asked the barmaid.
"Tiny," said the man.
"Why do you call him Tiny?"
"Because he's my newt!"

What do you get if you cross a nun
and a chicken?
A pecking order.

What does Luke Skywalker shave
with?
A laser blade.

Which capital city cheats at
exams?
Peking.

Why did the woman take a load of
hay to bed?
To feed her nightmare.

What happened when the wheel
was invented?
It caused a revolution.

Ivan: What are you reading?
Andrea: It's a book about
electricity.
Ivan: Oh, current events?
Andrea: No, light reading.

How did Benjamin Franklin
discover electricity?
It came to him in a flash.

Where do geologists go for
entertainment?
To rock concerts.

Why is history the sweetest
lesson?
Because it's full of dates.

What's wrong with this fish?
Long time, no sea.

What did the tie say to the hat?
You go on ahead and I'll hang
around.

What did the picture say to the
wall?
I've got you covered.

Why did the man take a pencil to bed?
To draw the curtains . . . I'd tell you another joke about a pencil, but it hasn't any point.

Why did the burglar take a shower?
He wanted to make a clean getaway.

Why do idiots eat biscuits?
Because they're crackers.

"What is your occupation?" asked
the magistrate.
"I'm a locksmith, your honor."
"And what were you doing in the
jeweler's shop at three in the
morning when the police officers
entered?"
"Making a bolt for the door!"

What do you call an American drawing?
Yankee Doodle.

A Dubliner was in court charged with parking his car in a restricted area. The judge asked if he had anything to say in his defense. "They shouldn't put up such misleading notices," said the Dubliner. "It said FINE FOR PARKING HERE."

What do you call an American with
a lavatory on his head?
John.

What's the name for a short-
legged tramp?
A low-down bum.

Why is it not safe to sleep on
trains?
Because they run over sleepers.

Sign in a cafe: All drinking water in this establishment has been personally passed by the management.

Did you hear about the farmer's boy who hated the country?
He went to the big city and got a job as a shoe-shine boy, and so the farmer made hay while the son shone!

"Gosh, it's raining cats and dogs," said Suzie looking out of the kitchen window.
"I know," said her mother who had just come in. "I've just stepped in a poodle!"

What did the Ancient Greeks shout when Archimedes fell in a dung-heap?
You Reeka! You Reeka!

Numbskulls

Why is the stupid red-headed boy
like a biscuit?
Because he's a ginger nut.

"How do you keep a stupid person
happy for hours?"
"Give him a piece of paper with
PTO written on both sides."

Did you hear about the man who hijacked a submarine?
He demanded a million dollars and a parachute.

When he received the end-of-term-report Brenda's father went crazy. "This report is terrible," he said, "I'm not at all pleased with it."
"I told the teacher you wouldn't like it," said Brenda, "but he insisted on sending it just the same."

A stupid glazier was examining a broken window. He looked at it for a while and then said: "It's worse than I thought. It's broken on both sides."

Why do stupid people eat biscuits? Because they're crackers.

Why did the robot act stupid? Because he had a screw loose.

My mother is so stupid that she
thinks a string quartet is four
people playing tennis.

A man telephoned London Airport.
"How long does it take to get to
New York?"
"Just a minute."
"Thanks very much."

My friend is so stupid that he
thinks twice before saying nothing.

Why did the stupid sailor grab a
bar of soap when his ship sank?
He thought he could wash himself
ashore.

Did you hear about the sailor that
was discharged from
the submarine service?
He was caught sleeping with the
windows open.

An idiotic laborer was told by an equally idiotic foreman to dig a hole in the road.

"And what shall I do with the earth, sir?" asked the laborer.

"Don't be daft, man," he replied. "Just dig another hole and bury it."

Did you hear about the stupid motorist who always drove his car in reverse?

It was because he knew the Highway Code backward."

A stupid bank robber rushed into a bank, pointed two fingers at the clerk and said: "This is a muck up."

"Don't you mean a stick up?" asked the girl.

"No," said the robber, "it's a muck up. I've forgotten my gun."

How do you confuse an idiot? Give him two spades and ask him to take his pick.

A stupid man spent the evening with some friends, but when the time came for him to leave, a terrific storm started with thunder, lightning and torrential rain. "You can't go home in this," said the host, "you'd better stay the night." "That's very kind of you," said the man, "I'll just pop home and get my pajamas."

A mountaineer fell down a very deep crevasse, breaking both his arms. Another member of the party managed to lower a rope until it was just within reach of the man's head.

"Quick!" he shouted. "Get hold of the rope with your teeth and I'll pull you up." Inch by painful inch, the mountaineer was dragged back up the crevasse. When he only had two feet to go, his rescuer called out, "Are you all right?"

"Yes, aaaaaaaaarrrrrrrggggghhhhhh!" came the reply.

Doctor: And did you drink your medicine after your bath, Mrs Soap?

Mrs Soap: No, doctor. By the time I'd drunk the bath there wasn't room for medicine.

Waiter, waiter, this lobster's only got one claw.

It must have been in a fight, sir.

Then bring me the winner.

My sister is so stupid she thinks that aroma is someone who travels a lot.

Did you hear about the idiot who won the Tour de France?
He did a lap of honor.

My friend is so stupid he thinks that an autograph is a chart showing sales figures for cars.

An idiot decided to start a chicken farm so he bought a hundred chickens to start. A month later he returned to the dealer for another hundred chickens because all of the first lot had died. A month later he was back at the dealers for another hundred chickens for the second lot had also died. "But I think I know where I'm going wrong," said the idiot. "I think I'm planting them too deep."

Why did the idiots' tug o' war
team lose the match?
They pushed.

My big brother is such an idiot.
The other day I saw him hitting
himself on the head with a
hammer. He was trying to make
his head swell so his hat wouldn't
fall over his eyes.

My sister is so dumb, she thinks
that a buttress is a female goat.

How does an idiot call for his dog?
He puts two fingers in his mouth
and then shouts Rover.

Did you hear about the idiotic
karate champion who joined the
army?
The first time he saluted, he
nearly killed himself.

Sandra's mother said no young man in his right mind would take her to the school dance in her bikini, so she decided to go with her friend's stupid brother.

Teacher: You weren't at school last Friday, Robert. I heard you were out playing football.
Robert: That's not true, Sir. And I've got the cinema tickets to prove it.

Did you hear about the utterly brainless monster who sat on the floor?
He fell off.

Did you hear about the idiot who had a new bath put in? The plumber said, "Would you like a plug for it?"
The idiot replied, "Oh, I didn't know it was electric."

Wally Woollynut was given the job of painting a flagpole but he didn't know how much paint he would need. "Lay it down and measure it," suggested a mate.
"That's no good," said Wally, "I need to know the height, not the length."

Did you hear what Dumb Donald did when he offered to paint the garage for his Dad in the summer holidays?
The instructions said "put on three coats," so he went in and put on his blazer, his raincoat and his duffel coat.

What's red, runs on wheels and eats grass?
A bus. I lied about the grass.

The math teacher and the English teacher went out for a quick pizza after school. "How long will the pizzas be?" asked the math teacher.

"Sorry, Sir," replied the waiter, "we don't do long pizzas, just ordinary round ones."

Wilberforce Witherspoon saw a notice outside a police station which read: MAN WANTED FOR ROBBERY. So he went in and applied for the job!

Simple Simon was writing a geography essay. It began, "The people who live in Paris are called parasites . . ."

My dad is stupid. He thinks a fjord is a Norwegian motor car.

Jimmy, how many more times must I tell you to come away from that biscuit barrel?
No more, mom. It's empty.

Did you hear about the stupid
photographer?
He saved burned-out lightbulbs
for use in his darkroom.

Did you hear about the village idiot
buying bird seed?
He said he wanted to grow some
birds.

I can't understand the critics saying that only an idiot would like that television program. I really enjoyed it.

Father: Would you like a pocket calculator for Christmas, son?
Danny: No thanks, Dad. I know how many pockets I've got.

Did you hear about the stupid tap dancer?
He fell in the sink.

At the scene of a bank raid the police sergeant came running up to his inspector and said, "He got away, sir!"
The inspector was furious. "But I told you to put a man on all the exits!" he roared. "How could he have got away?"
"He left by one of the entrances, sir!"

A stupid man was struggling out of his house with a big table. His neighbor said to him, "Hello, Harry. Where are you going with that then?"

And Harry replied, "I'm taking it to the draper's shop to have it measured for a new tablecloth."

On their first evening in their new home the bride went in to the kitchen to fix the drinks. Five minutes later she came back into the living-room in tears.

"What's the matter, my angel?" asked her husband anxiously.

"Oh Derek!" she sobbed, "I put the ice cubes in hot water to wash them and now they've disappeared!"

A doctor had been attending a rich old man for some time, but it became apparent that the old chap had not long to live. Accordingly, the doctor advised his wealthy patient to put his affairs in order. "Oh yes, I've done that," said the old gentleman. "I've only got to make my will. And do you know what I'm going to do with all my money? I'm going to leave it to the doctor who saves my life . . ."

Vincent, why have you got a sausage stuck behind your ear? Eh? Oh no, I must have eaten my pencil for lunch!

A man rushed into the doctor's surgery, jumped on the doctor's back, and started screaming "One! Two! Three! Four!"
"Wait a minute!" yelled the doctor, struggling to free himself. "What do you think you're doing?"
"Well, doctor," said the eccentric man, "they did say I could count on you!"

The criminal mastermind found one of his gang sawing the legs off his bed. "What are you doing that for?" demanded the crook boss.

"Only doing what you ordered," said the stupid thug. "You told me to lie low for a bit!"

A jeweler standing behind the counter of his shop was astounded to see a man come hurtling head-first through the window.

"What on earth are you up to?" he demanded.

"I'm terribly sorry," said the man, "I forgot to let go of the brick!"

John kept pestering his parents to buy a video, but they said they couldn't afford one. So one day John came home clutching a package containing a brand-new video. "Wherever did you get the money to pay for that?" asked his father suspiciously.

"It's all right, Dad," replied John, "I traded the TV in for it."

Classroom Jokes

Alec turned up for football practice clutching a large broom.
"What's that for?" asked the coach.
"You said I was going to be sweeper today."

"Teacher is a bore!" was scrawled on the blackboard one day.
"I do not want to see that on my blackboard," he thundered when he saw it.
"Sorry, Sir! I didn't realize you wanted it kept secret."

"Ann! Point out Australia for me on the map."

Ann went to the front of the class, picked up the pointer and showed the rest of the class where Australia was.

"Well done! Now, Alec! Can you tell us who discovered Australia?"

"Er . . . Ann, Miss?"

"And what might your name be?"
the school secretary asked the
new boy.
"Well it might be Cornelius, but it's
not. It's Sam."

What happens if there's a collision
outside school?
There's usually a fight.

What happened to the baby chicken that misbehaved at school?
It was eggspelled.

Teacher: I was going to read you a story called "The Invasion of the Body Snatchers," but I've changed my mind.
Class: Oh why, Miss?
Teacher: Because we might get carried away.

"Ann," said the dancing mistress. "There are two things stopping you becoming the world's greatest ballerina?"
"What are they, Miss?" asked Ann.
"Your feet."

"I hope you're not one of those boys who sits and watches the school clock," said the principal to a new boy.
"No, Sir. I've got a digital watch that bleeps at half past three."

What's the definition of a school report?
A poison pen letter from the principal.

Why did the soccer teacher give his team lighters?
Because they kept losing all their matches.

What's the difference between school dinners and a bucket of fresh manure?
School dinners are usually cold.

Did you hear about the cross-eyed teacher who had no control over her pupils?

What's the longest piece of furniture in the school?
The multiplication table.

What do you get if you cross old
potatoes with lumpy mince?
School dinners.

Miss Jones who teaches us maths,
Isn't a bundle of laughs.
For, sad to tell,
She doesn't half smell,
For she never seems to take any
baths.

Did you hear about the teacher
who married the dairy maid?
It didn't last. They were like chalk
and cheese.

"Why are you crying Amanda?"
asked her teacher.
" 'Cos Jenny's broken my new doll,
Miss," she cried.
"How did she do that?"
"I hit her on the head with it."

Did you hear about the teacher who retired?
His class gave him an illuminated address. They burned his house down.

Confucius he say: If teacher ask you question and you not know answer, mumble.

What did the arithmetic book say to the geometry book?
Boy! Do we have our problems!

"And what's your name?" the secretary asked the next new boy.
"Butter."
"I hope your first name's not Roland," smirked the secretary.
"No, Miss. It's Brendan."

"What's your first name?" the teacher asked a new boy.
It's Orson, Miss. I was named after Orson Wells, the film star."
"Just as well your last name's not Cart. Isn't it?"
"Yes Miss. It's Trapp."

Did you hear about the math
teacher who fainted in class?
Everyone tried to bring her 2.

A little girl was next in line. "My
name's Curtain," she said.
"I hope your first name's not
Annette?"
"No. It's Velvet."

What's the difference between a boring teacher and a boring book? You can shut the book up.

Teacher: That's the stupidest boy in the whole school.
Mother: That's my son.
Teacher: Oh! I'm so sorry.
Mother: You're sorry?

"Oh I'm sorry. I didn't realize you were her mother.

"I'm not. I'm her father actually! And she's my son!"

Typing teacher: Bob! Your work has certainly improved. There are only ten mistakes here.

Bob: Oh good, Miss.

Teacher: Now let's look at the second line, shall we?

A teacher in a country school received the following letter from the mother of one of his students:

Dear Teacher,

Please excuse Phil from school last week. His father was ill and the pig had to be fed.

Yours sincerely,

Why are art galleries like retirement homes for teachers? Because they're both full of old masters.

It was sweltering hot outside. The teacher came into the classroom wiping his brow and said, "Ninety-two today. Ninety-two."

"Happy birthday to you. Happy birthday to you. . ." sang the class.

Did you hear about the brilliant geography master?

He had abroad knowledge of his subject.

"What's your father's occupation?" asked the school secretary on the first day of the new term.

"He's a conjurer, Miss," said the new boy.

"How interesting. What's his favorite trick?"

"He saws people in half."

"Golly! Now next question. Any brothers and sisters?"

"One half-brother and two half-sisters."

Billy's mother was called into the school one day by the principal. "We're very worried about Billy," he said. "He goes round all day 'cluck, cluck, clucking'."

"That's right," said Billy's mother. "He thinks he's a chicken."

"Haven't you taken him to a psychiatrist?"

"Well we would, but we need the eggs."

Two elderly teachers were talking over old times and saying how much things had changed. "I mean," said the first, "I caught one of the boys kissing one of the girls yesterday."

"Extraordinary," said the second. "I didn't even kiss my wife before I married her, did you?"

"I can't remember. What was her maiden name?"

"Please Sir. There's something wrong with my stomach."
"Well button up your jacket and no one will notice."

"Now remember boys and girls," said the science teacher. "You can tell a tree's age by counting the rings in a cross section. One ring for each year."
Alec went home for tea and found a Swiss Roll on the table.
"I'm not eating that, Mom," he said. "It's five years old."

Did you hear about the schoolboy
who just couldn't get to grips with
decimals?
He couldn't see the point.

A warning to any young sinner,
Be you fat or perhaps even thinner.
If you do not repent,
To Hell you'll be sent.
With nothing to eat but school
dinner.

A mother was desperate to get her under-age daughter into kindergarten and was trying to impress the headmistress with the child's intellectual abilities. "She'll easily keep up with the others even though she is a year younger."

"Well," said the teacher doubtfully. "Could she prove it by saying something?"

"Certainly Miss," said the child. "Something pertaining to your conversation, or something purely irrelevant?"

100

Why did the science teacher marry
the school cleaner?
Because she swept him off his
feet.

How do Religious Education
teachers mark exams?
With spirit levels.

Teacher's strong; teacher's gentle.
Teacher's kind. And I am mental.

Please Sir! Please Sir! Why do you
keep me locked up in this cage?
Because you're the teacher's pet.

Teacher: Are you good at arithmetic?
Mary: Well, yes and no.
Teacher: What do you mean, yes and no?
Mary: Yes, I'm no good at arithmetic.

Why is a pencil the heaviest thing in your satchel
Because it's full of lead.

Mrs Jones: Well, Billy, how are you getting along with the trampolining in PE?

Billy: Oh, up and down, you know.

Mandy: Our teacher went on a special banana diet.

Andy: Did she lose weight?

Mandy: No, but she couldn't half climb trees well!

Art Teacher: What color would you paint the sun and the wind?

Brian: The sun rose, and the wind blue.

Teacher: Your books are a disgrace, Archibald. I don't see how anyone can possibly make as many mistakes in one day as you do.

Archibald: I get here early, Sir.

When is an English teacher like a judge?
When she hands out long sentences.

Geography Teacher: What mineral do we import from America?
Daft Darren: Coca-Cola!

What's black and white and horrible?
A math examination paper.

What nickname did the police give to the new blonde woman police officer?
A fair cop.

Kelly: Is God a doctor, Miss?
Teacher: In some ways, Kelly. Why do you ask?
Kelly: Because the Bible says that the Lord gave the tablets to Moses.

How can you tell when it's rabbit pie
for school dinner?
It has hares in it.

George knocked on the door of his
friend's house. When his friend's
mother answered he said: "Can
Albert come out to play?"
"No, said the mother, "it's too
cold."
"Well, then," said George "can his
football come out to play?"

What is brown, hairy, wears dark glasses and carries a pile of exercise books?
A coconut disguised as a teacher.

Why did the teacher put corn in his shoes?
Because he had pigeon toes.

What do you call a deaf teacher?
Anything you like, he can't hear you.

How can a teacher double his money?
By folding it in half.

Teacher: What is a Red Indian's home called?
Andy: I don't know, Miss, but I know what a little Red Indian's joke is called.
Teacher: Well, what is it called?
Andy: A Minihaha.

Girl: My teacher's a peach.
Mother: You mean she's sweet.
Girl: No, she has a heart of stone.

Headmaster: I've called you into my office, Peter, because I want to talk to you about two words I wish you wouldn't use so often. One is "great" and the other is "lousy."
Peter: Certainly Sir. What are they?

Mother: How was your first day at school?

Little Boy: OK, but I haven't got my present yet.

Mother: What do you mean?

Little Boy: Well the teacher gave me a chair, and said "Sit there for the present."

Teacher to pupil: How many thousand times have I told you not to exaggerate?

Father: Jennifer, I've had a letter from your principal. It seems you've been neglecting your appearance.

Jennifer: Dad?

Father: He says you haven't appeared in school all week.

Teacher: What happened to your homework?

Boy: I made it into a paper plane and someone hijacked it.

Tom: Why are you scratching your head?

Harry: I've got those arithmetic bugs again.

Tom: Arithmetic bugs – what are they?

Harry: Well, some people call them head lice.

Tom: "Then why do you call them arithmetic bugs?"

Harry: "Because they add to my misery, subtract from my pleasure, divide my attention and multiply like crazy."

Teacher: What's the best way to pass this geometry test?
Boy: Knowing all the angles?

Teacher: You should have been here at nine o'clock.
Boy: Why? Did something happen?

Mother: What did you learn at school today?
Son: Not enough. I have to go back tomorrow.

Teacher: If I had ten flies on my desk, and I swatted one, how many flies would be left?
Girl: One – the dead one!

One unfortunate teacher started off a lesson with the following instruction, "I want you all to give me a list of the lower animals, starting with Georgina Clark . . ."

Music master: Brian, if "f" means forte, what does "ff" mean?
Brian: Eighty!

"Frank," said the weary math teacher, "if you had seven dollars in your pocket, and seven dollars in another pocket, what would you have?"
"Someone else's trousers on!"

Teacher: Martin, I've taught you everything I know, and you're still ignorant!

Teacher: Ford, you're late for school again. What is it this time?
Ford: I sprained my ankle, sir.
Teacher: That's a lame excuse.

Creatures Great and Small

A woodpecker was pecking a hole in a tree. All of a sudden a flash of lightning struck the tree to the ground. The woodpecker looked bemused for a moment and then said: "Gee, I guess I don't know my own strength."

What do you get it you cross a hedgehog with a giraffe?
A long-necked toothbrush.

There was once a puppy called May who loved to pick quarrels with animals who were bigger than she was. One day she argued with a lion. The next day was the first of June.
Why? Because that was the end of May!

What kind of cats love water?
Octopusses.

Why does a stork stand on one
leg?
Because it would fall over if it
lifted the other one.

First flea: You don't look too well.
Second flea: I'm not really feeling
up to scratch.

My dog saw a sign that said: "Wet
Paint" – so he did!

What's a porcupine's favorite food?
Prickled onions.

My dog is a nuisance. He chases
everyone on a bicycle. What can I
do?
Take his bike away.

What's an American cat's favorite
car?
A Catillac.

What's black and white and makes
a lot of noise?
A zebra with a set of drums.

What is a snail?
A slug with a crash helmet.

What should you do if you find a
gorilla sitting at your school desk?
Sit somewhere else.

What did the stupid ghost call his
pet tiger?
Spot.

Teacher: Who can tell me what
geese eat?
Paul: Er, gooseberries, Sir?

What were the only creatures not to
go into the ark in pairs?
Maggots. They went in an apple.

Why should a school not be near a chicken farm?
To avoid the pupils overhearing fowl language.

Teacher: Martin, put some more water in the fish tank.
Martin: But, Sir, they haven't drunk the water I gave them yesterday.

Mary had a bionic cow,
It lived on safety pins.
And every time she milked that cow
The milk came out in tins.

What do you get if you pour hot water down a rabbit hole?
Hot cross bunnies!

What do you get if you cross a galaxy with a toad?
Star Warts.

On which side does a chicken
have the most feathers?
On the outside.

Which bird is always out of breath?
A puffin.

What's the best thing to give a
seasick elephant?
Plenty of room.

What sort of fish performs
surgical operations?
A sturgeon.

Just before the Ark set sail, Noah
saw his two sons fishing over the
side. "Go easy on the bait, lads,"
he said. "Remember I've only got
two worms."

What's a twip?
What a wabbit calls a twain ride!

Baby Skunk: But, Mom, why can't I have a chemistry set for my birthday?
Mother: Because it would stink the house out, that's why.

Waiter, waiter, there's a dead beetle in my gravy.
Yes, sir. Beetles are terrible swimmers.

Keith: Our teacher's an old bat.
Kevin: You mean he's bad-
tempered?
Keith: Not only that, he hangs
around us all the time.

A teacher took her class for a walk
in the country, and Susie found a
grass snake. "Come quickly,
Miss," she called, "here's a tail
without a body!"

The Stock Market is a place where sheep and cattle are sold.

How do you catch a squirrel?
Climb up a tree and act like a nut.

Which animals do you have to beware of when you take exams?
Cheetahs.

Why did the elephant paint her
head yellow?
To see if blondes really do have
more fun.

How many skunks does it take to
make a big stink?
A phew!

What was the fly doing in the
alphabet soup?
Learning to spell.

What happened when the headmistress's poodle swallowed a roll of film?
Nothing serious developed.

What did the neurotic pig say to the farmer?
You take me for grunted.

What did the beaver say to the tree?
It sure is good to gnaw you.

Why don't centipedes play football?
Because by the time they've got
their boots on it's time to go home.

What's the difference between a
coyote and a flea?
One howls on the prairie, and the
other prowls on the hairy.

Donald: My canary died of 'flu.
Dora: I didn't know canaries got
'flu.
Donald: Mine flew into a car.

How do fleas travel from place to place?
By itch hiking.

What do you get if you cross a yeti with a kangaroo?
A fur coat with big pockets.

What do you get if you cross a cow and a camel?
Lumpy milkshakes!

What do you get if you cross a
sheep-dog and a bunch of
daisies?
Collie-flowers!

What do you get if you cross a
zebra and a donkey?
A zeedonk.

What do you get if you cross a
sheep and a rainstorm?
A wet blanket.

There were two mosquitoes
watching blood donors giving their
blood. "It's not fair," said one to the
other. "They're happy to lie down
and let someone drain a pint of
blood, but if we zoomed down for a
quick nip, they'd do their best to
kill us."

An elephant ran away from a circus and ended up in a little old lady's back garden. The lady had never seen an elephant before, so she rang the police.

"Please come quickly," she said to the policeman who answered the phone. "There's a strange looking animal in my garden picking up cabbages with its tail."

"What's it doing with them?" asked the policeman.

"If I told you," said the old lady, "you'd never believe me!"

What do you get if you cross a centipede and a parrot?
A walkie-talkie.

Two caterpillars were crawling along a twig when a butterfly flew by. "You know," said one caterpillar to the other, "when I grow up, you'll never get me in one of those things."

What dog smells of onions?
A hot dog.

What lies on the ground 100 feet
up in the air and smells?
A dead centipede.

What did the grape do when the
elephant sat on it?
It let out a little wine.

What do you call a flea that lives in
an idiot's ear?
A space invader.

What do ants take when they are
ill?
Antibiotics.

Who conquered half the world,
laying eggs along the way?
Attila the Hen.

When is it bad luck to be followed
by a black cat?
When you're a mouse.

The psychiatrist was surprised to see a tortoise come into his office. "What can I do for you, Mr Tortoise?" asked the psychiatrist. "I'm terribly shy, doctor," said the tortoise, "I want you to cure me of that." "No problem. I'll soon have you out of your shell."

Why was the young kangaroo thrown out by his mother? For smoking in bed.

Two fish were swimming in a stream when it began to rain. "Quick," said one fish to the other, "let's swim under that bridge, otherwise we'll get wet!"

"Who's been eating my porridge?" squeaked Baby Bear.
"Who's been eating my porridge?" cried Mother Bear.
"Burp!" said Father Bear.

Why are skunks always arguing?
'Cos they like to raise a stink.

If twenty dogs run after one dog,
what time is it?
Twenty after one.

Rabbits can multipy – but only a
snake can be an adder.

How did Noah see to the animals
in the Ark?
By flood-lighting.

What swings through trees and is
very dangerous?
A chimpanzee with a machine-
gun.

What has four legs, whiskers, a
tail, and flies?
A dead cat.

Have you ever seen a man-eating tiger?
No, but in the cafe next door I once saw a man eating chicken!

First cat: How did you get on in the milk-drinking contest?
Second cat: Oh, I won by six laps!

A man who bought a dog took it back, complaining that it made a mess all over the house. "I thought you said it was house-trained," he moaned.

"So it is," said the previous owner. "It won't go anywhere else."

Sign in shop window:
FOR SALE Pedigree bulldog. House trained. Eats anything. Very fond of children.

Why couldn't the butterfly go to
the dance?
Because it was a moth-ball.

What do you get if you cross a flea
with a rabbit?
Bugs Bunny.

What do you get if you cross a
crocodile with a flower?
I don't know, but I'm not going to
smell it.

What do you call a multi-story
pig-pen?
A styscraper.

How can you tell if an elephant has
been sleeping in your bed?
The sheets are wrinkled and the
bed smells of peanuts.

Did you hear about the boy who sat
under a cow?
He got a pat on the head.

Why do elephants have flat feet?
From jumping out of tall trees.

Is the squirt from an elephant's
trunk very powerful?
Of course – a jumbo jet can keep
500 people in the air for hours at a
time.

How do you make an elephant
sandwich?
First of all you get a very large
loaf...

Mean and Nasty Jokes

The garbage men were just about to leave the street when a woman came running out of the house carrying some cardboard boxes.
"Am I too late for the garbage?" she called.
"No, lady," replied one of the men. "Jump right in!"

Girl: Did you like that cake Mrs Jones?
Mrs Jones: Yes, very much.
Girl: That's funny. My mom said you didn't have any taste.

A woman woke her husband in the middle of the night. "There's a burglar downstairs eating the cake that I made this morning."

"Who shall I call," her husband said, "Police or ambulance?"

Fred: I was sorry to hear that your mother-in-law had died. What was the complaint?

Ted: We haven't had any yet.

When you leave school, you should become a bone specialist. You've certainly got the head for it.

My auntie Maud had so many candles on her last birthday cake that all her party guests got sunburnt.

When Wally Witherspoon proposed
to his girlfriend she said:
"I love the simple things in life,
Wally, but I don't want one of them
for a husband."

Two friends were discussing the
latest scandalous revelations
about a Hollywood actress.
"They say she likes her latest
husband so much she's decided to
keep him for another month," said
one to the other.

Roger was in a very full bus when a fat woman opposite said, "If you were a gentleman, young man, you'd stand up and let someone else sit down."

"And if you were a lady," replied Roger, "you'd stand up and let four people sit down."

My son's just received a scholarship to medical school – but they don't want him while he's alive.

My Mother uses lemon juice for her complexion. Maybe that is why she always looks so sour.

My auntie Mabel has got so many double chins it looks like she is peering over a pile of crumpets.

Chuck: Do you have holes in your underpants?
Teacher: No, of course not.
Chuck: Then how do you get your feet through?

My girlfriend talks so much that when she goes on holiday, she has to spread suntan lotion on her tongue.

At my piano teacher's last performance the audience cheered and cheered. The piano was locked!

A school inspector was talking to a pupil. "How many teachers work in this school?" he asked.
"Only about half of them, I reckon," replied the pupil.

Father: Would you like me to help you with your homework?
Son: No thanks, I'd rather get it wrong by myself.

I wouldn't say our English teacher is fat, but when she got on a Speak Your Weight machine it surrendered.

Rob: I must rush home and cut the lawn.
Teacher: Did your father promise you something if you cut it?
Rob: No, he promised me something if I didn't!

She's such a gossip she tells you what you were going to say to her before you have the chance to tell her.

I have two noses, three eyes and only one ear. What am I?
Very ugly.

Mrs Broadbeam: Now, remember, children, travel is very good for you. It broadens the mind.
Sarah, muttering: If you're anything to go by, that's not all it broadens!

Why is a caretaker nothing like Robinson Crusoe?
Because Robinson Crusoe got all his work done by Friday.

"Did you see him?" asked the policeman.
"No," said Mrs Blenkinsop, "but I'd know that laugh anywhere."

I can't get over that new beard of yours. It makes your face look just like a busted sofa.

Henry: I'd like to learn to play a drum, Sir.
Music Teacher: Beat it!

What do you get if you pour boiling water down a rabbit hole?
Hot cross bunnies.

Yes, I do like your dress — but isn't it a little early for Hallowe'en?

You must think I'm a perfect idiot.
No, you're not perfect.

Soprano at concert: And what would you like me to sing next?
Member of audience: Do you know "Old Man River"?
Soprano: Er, yes.
Member of audience: Well go jump in it.

I don't care who you are, get those reindeer off my roof.

I don't know what it is that makes you stupid but whatever it is, it works.

My dad is rather tired this morning. Last night he dreamed he was working.

Wife: Shall I give that tramp one of my cakes?
Husband: Why, what harm has he ever done us?

My uncle spent a fortune on deodorants before he found out that people didn't like him anyway.

What is small, pink, wrinkly, and belongs to Grandpa?
Grandma.

Why don't you go home and brush
up on your ignorance?

How does your head feel today?
As good as new.
It should be as good as new – it's
never been used.

My uncle must be the meanest
man in the world. He recently
found a crutch – then he broke his
leg so he could use it.

I've got a good idea.
Must be beginner's luck.

I reckon mom must be at least 30
years old – I counted the rings
under her eyes.

Woman: If you were my husband
I'd poison your coffee.
Man: And if you were my wife, I'd
drink it.

Visitor: You're very quiet, Jennifer.
Jennifer: Well, my mom gave me 10 cents not to say anything about your red nose.

Mom! There's a man at the door collecting for the Old Folks' Home. Shall I give him Grandma?

I've just finished painting your portrait. There, don't you think it looks like you?
Er . . . well . . . it probably looks better from a distance.
"I told you it was like you!"

The new office-boy came into his boss's office and said, "I think you're wanted on the phone, sir."
"What d'you mean, you think?" demanded the boss.
"Well, sir, the phone rang, I answered it and a voice said, 'Is that you, you old fool?'"

Billy: I never had a sledge when I was a kid. We were too poor.

Milly, feeling sorry for him: What a shame! What did you do when it snowed?

Billy: Slid down the hills on my cousin.

Do you think, Professor, that my wife should take up the piano as a career?

No, I think she should put down the lid as a favor.

Why did you refuse to marry
Richard, Tessa?
'Cos he said he would die if I
didn't and I'm just curious.

My Peter keeps telling everyone
he's going to marry the most
beautiful girl in the world.
What a shame! And after all the
time you've been engaged!

Doctor Sawbones speaking.
Oh, doctor, my wife's just
dislocated her jaw. Can you come
over in, say, three or four weeks
time?

"How should I have played that
last shot?" the bad golfer asked
his partner.
"Under an assumed name."

May I go swimming, Mommy?
No, you may not. There are sharks
here.
But Daddy's swimming.
He's insured.

Alfie had been listening to his
sister practice her singing. "Sis,"
he said, "I wish you'd sing
Christmas carols."
"That's nice of you Alfie," she said,
"why?"
"Then I'd only have to hear you
once a year!"

A rather stern aunt had been
staying with Sharon's parents, and
one day she said to the little girl,
"Well, Sharon, I'm going tomorrow.
Are you sorry?"
"Oh yes, Auntie," replied Sharon.
"I thought you were going today."

A scoutmaster asked one of his
troop what good deed he had
done for the day. "Well Skip," said
the scout. "Mom had only one
dose of castor oil left, so I let my
baby brother have it."

The apprentice electrician was on his first job. "Take hold of those two wires, Alex," said his master, "and rub them together."

Alex did as he was bid, and his master said, "Do you feel anything?"

"No," said Alex.

"That's good – so don't touch those other two wires or you'll get a nasty shock!"

A naughty child was irritating all the passengers on the flight from London to New York. Finally, one man could stand it no longer. "Hey kid," he shouted, "why don't you go outside and play?"

Mr Brown: I hate to tell you, but your wife just fell in the wishing well.
Mr Smith: It works!

Did you hear about the woman who was so ugly she could make yogurt by staring at a pint of milk for an hour?

"Some girls think I'm handsome," said the young Romeo, "and some girls think I'm ugly. What do you think, Sheila?"
"A bit of both. Pretty ugly."

You're ugly!
And you're drunk!
Yes, but in the morning I'll be
sober!

I don't think these photographs
you've taken do me justice.
You don't want justice – you want
mercy!

Food and Physical Jokes

Jane's father decided to take all the family out to a restaurant for a meal. As he'd spent quite a lot of money for the meal he said to the waiter, "Could I have a bag to take the leftovers home for the dog?" "Gosh!" exclaimed Jane, "are we getting a dog?"

Why is it that when I stand on my head the blood rushes to my head but when I stand on my feet the blood doesn't rush to my feet? You're feet aren't empty.

A fat girl went into a cafe and ordered two slices of apple pie with four scoops of ice cream covered with lashings of raspberry sauce and piles of chopped nuts. "Would you like a cherry on the top?" asked the waitress.

"No, thanks," said the girl, "I'm on a diet."

Mom: Eat up your roast beef, it's full of iron.

Dottie: No wonder it's so tough.

A woman telephoned her local newspaper to let them know that she had just given birth to eighteen children. The reporter didn't quite hear the message and said, "Would you repeat that?"
"Not if I can help it," replied the woman.

Neil: I've changed my mind.
Jim: About time, too. Does the new one work any better?

You should get a job in the
meteorology office.
Why?
Because you're an expert on wind.

That boy is so dirty, the only time
he washes his ears is when he
eats watermelon.

Waiter, how long have you worked here?

Six months, Sir.

Well, it can't have been you who took my order.

What happened to Lady Godiva's horse when he realized that she wasn't wearing any clothes?

It made him shy.

Doctor, doctor, I think I'm a spoon.
Sit over there, please, and don't
stir.

Doctor, doctor, my son's just
swallowed some gunpowder!
Well, don't point him at me.

Doctor, doctor, I'm at death's door!
Don't worry, Mrs Jenkins. An
operation will soon pull you
through.

Doctor, doctor, Cuthbert keeps
biting his nails!
That's not serious in a child.
But Cuthbert bites his toenails.

Doctor: Good morning, Mrs
Feather. Haven't seen you for a
long time.
Mrs Feather: I know, doctor. It's
because I've been ill.

Why did the farmer plow his field
with a steamroller?
Because he planned to grow
mashed potatoes.

Doctor, I keep stealing things.
What can I do?
Try to resist the temptation, but if
you can't, get me a new television.

Nicky and Vicky were talking about a famous, very glamorous film star. "What do you think of her clothes?" asked Nicky.

"I'd say they were chosen to bring out the bust in her," replied Vicky.

How did the baker get an electric shock?

He stood on a bun and a current ran up his leg.

Did you hear about Lenny the Loafer? He is so lazy that he sticks his nose out of the window so that the wind will blow it for him.

Doctor, doctor, how can I stop my cold going to my chest?
Tie a knot in your neck.

Doctor, doctor I keep losing my memory.
When did you first notice that?
When did I first notice what?

Some people say the school cook's cooking is out of this world.
Most pupils wish it was out of their stomachs.

Waiter, waiter, why is my apple pie all mashed up?
You did ask me to step on it, sir.

Do men always snore?
Only when they are asleep.

What did the dinner lady say when
the teacher told her off for putting
her finger in his soup?
It's all right, it isn't hot.

Brian: How did you manage to get
a black eye?
Bertie: You see that tree in the
playground?
Brian: Yes.
Bertie: Well, I didn't.

Waiter, waiter, have you got frogs'
legs?
No Sir, I always walk like this.

Ben, sniffing: Smells like UFO for
dinner tonight, chaps.
Ken: What's UFO?
Ben: Unidentified Frying Objects.

Statistics say that one in three people is mentally ill. So check your friends and if two of them seem okay, you're the one.

Doctor, doctor, my wife thinks she's a duck.
You better bring her in to see me straight away.
I can't do that – she's already flown south for the winter.

What kind of beans do cannibals
like best?
Human beans.

Doctor, doctor, I think I'm invisible.
Who said that?

Did you hear about the two fat
men who ran in the New York
Marathon?
One ran in short bursts, the other
in burst shorts!

Did you hear about the dentist
who became a brain surgeon?
His drill slipped.

What do traffic wardens like for tea?
Traffic jam sandwiches.

Cannibal Boy: I've brought a friend home for dinner.
Cannibal Mom: Put him in the fridge and we'll have him tomorrow.

What is a dimple?
A pimple going the wrong way.

What happened to the man who put his false teeth in backwards? He ate himself!

What is the most popular food served at a nudist camp? Skinless sausages.

What's the best thing to put into a pizza? Your teeth.

Ronald had broken a rib playing rugby. He went to the doctor, who asked how he was feeling. "I keep getting a stitch in my side," he replied.

"That's good," said the doctor. "It shows the bone is knitting."

A man who tests people's eyes is called an optimist.

Why did the old lady cover her mouth with her hands when she sneezed?
To catch her false teeth.

There was a fight in the fish shop last night – a whole lot of fish got battered!

Doctor, doctor, I keep seeing double.
Take a seat, please.
Which one?

What kind of jokes does a
chiropodist like?
Corny jokes.

Doctor, doctor, I think I've been
bitten by a vampire.
Drink this glass of water.
Will it make me better?
No, but I'll be able to see if your
neck leaks.

Which vegetable goes best with
jacket potatoes?
Button mushrooms.

How can you tell an old person
from a young person?
An old person can sing and brush
their teeth at the same time.

My auntie has a sore throat. What
should she do?
Take aunti-septic.

Who's stronger than a muscleman
who can tear up a telephone
directory?
Someone who can tear up a street.

Ben's new girlfriend uses such greasy lipstick that he has to sprinkle his face with sand to get a better grip.

Waiter: And how did you find your meat, sir?
Customer: Oh, I just lifted a potato and there it was.

Why are fried onions like a photocopying machine?
They keep repeating themselves.

What happens if you tell a psychiatrist you are schizophrenic? He charges you double.

The kidneys are infernal organs.

Doctor, doctor, it's wonderful! I feel like my old self again.
In that case we'd better start a new course of treatment.

Doctor, doctor, I've only got fifty
seconds to live.
Just sit over there a minute.

Did you hear about the girl who
got engaged to a chap and then
found out he had a wooden leg?
She broke it off, of course . . .

Why did the orange stop rolling
down the hill?
It ran out of juice.

My uncle's got a wooden leg.
That's nothing. My auntie has a
wooden chest.

How do you make gold soup?
Use fourteen carats.

Waiter, waiter, there's a bird in my
soup.
That's all right, sir. It's bird-nest
soup.

Waiter, waiter, this coffee tastes
like mud.
I'm not surprised, sir, it was ground
only a few minutes ago.

"I'm sorry," said the surgeon. "But
I left a sponge in you when I
operated last week."
"Oh," said the patient, "I was
wondering why I was so thirsty all
the time."

"Ugh! You smell terrible," said a doctor to a patient.

"That's odd," said the patient, "that's what the other doctor said."

"If you were told that by another doctor, why have you come to me?"

"Because I wanted a second opinion."

Trevor came rushing in to his dad. "Dad," he puffed, "is it true that an apple a day keeps the doctor away?"

"That's what they say," said his dad.

"Well, give us an apple quick – I've just broken the doctor's window!"

Jimmy was caught by his mother in the pantry. "And what do you think you're up to?" she asked furiously.

"I'm up to my seventh jelly tart," said Jimmy.

Now then, Deirdre, eat up all your greens like a good girl. They're good for your complexion, you know.
But I don't want to have a green complexion.

A tramp knocked on the back door of a house and asked for a bite to eat.
"Go away," said the lady of the house, "I never feed tramps."
"That's all right lady," said the tramp, "I'll feed myself."

"The trouble is," said the entertainer to the psychiatrist, "that I can't sing; I can't dance; I can't tell jokes; I can't act; I can't play an instrument or juggle or do magic tricks or do anything!"

"Then why don't you give up show-business?"

"I can't – I'm a star!"

Doctor, doctor! I'm becoming invisible!

Yes, I can see you're not all there.

A man sat on a train chewing gum and staring vacantly into space, when suddenly an old woman sitting opposite said, "It's no good you talking to me, young man, I'm stone deaf!"

Doctor, doctor! You've taken out my tonsils, my adenoids, my gall-bladder, my varicose veins and my appendix, but I still don't feel well. That's quite enough out of you.

Little Jackie's mother was on the telephone to the boy's dentist. "I don't understand it," she complained, "I thought his treatment would only cost me $10, but you've charged me $40." "It is usually $10, madam," agreed the dentist, "but Jackie yelled so loudly that three of my other patients ran away!"

Three men were in the dock, and the judge, who had a terrible squint, said to the first, "How do you plead?"

"Not guilty," said the second.

"I'm not talking to you," snapped the judge.

"I didn't say a word," said the third.

Fantasy
Figures

Did you hear about the monster
who ate bits of metal every night?
It was his staple diet.

If a flying saucer is an aircraft,
does that make a flying
broomstick a witchcraft?

How do you get a ghost to lie
perfectly flat?
You use a spirit level.

What do you call a ghost who only haunts the Town Hall?
The nightmayor.

Monster: Stick 'em down.
Ghost: Don't you mean, stick 'em up?
Monster: No wonder I'm not making much money in this business.

What do you call a skeleton who goes out in the snow and rain without a coat or an umbrella? A numbskull.

What did the werewolf eat after he'd had his teeth taken out? The dentist.

Mommy, mommy, what's a vampire? Be quiet, dear, and drink your soup before it clots.

Why don't ghosts make good magicians?
You can see right through their tricks.

Ghost: Are you coming to my party?
Spook: Where is it?
Ghost: In the morgue – you know what they say, the morgue the merrier.

What did Frankenstein's monster say when he was struck by lightning?
"Thanks, I needed that."

What did E.T's mother say to him when he got home?
Where on Earth have you been?

What do you get if you cross a zombie with a boy scout?
A creature that scares old ladies across the road.

Did the bionic monster have a brother?
No, but he had lots of trans-sisters.

The ghost teacher was giving her pupils instructions on how to haunt a house properly. "Has everyone got the hang of walking through walls?" she asked. One little ghoul at the front of the class looked uncertain.
"Just watch the blackboard everyone," instructed the teacher, "and I'll go through it once more."

225

Where does Dracula keep his savings?
In the blood bank.

Igor: Only this morning Dr Frankenstein completed another amazing operation. He crossed an ostrich with a centipede.
Dracula: And what did he get?
Igor: We don't know – we haven't managed to catch it yet.

Did you hear about the monster
who was known as Captain Kirk?
He had a left ear, a right ear and a
final front ear.

A monster decided to become a TV
star, so he went to see an agent.
"What do you do?" asked the
agent.
"Bird impressions," said the
monster.
"What kind of bird impressions?"
"I eat worms."

Did you hear about the skeleton
which was attacked by the dog?
It ran off with some bones and left
him without a leg to stand on.

What did the werewolf write at the
bottom of the letter?
Best vicious . . .

What happened when the werewolf
met the five-headed monster?
It was love at first fright.

A monster walked into a shop selling dress fabrics and said, "I'd like six meters of pink satan for my wife."

"It's satin, sir, not satan," said the assistant. "Satan is something that looks like the devil."

"Oh," said the monster, "you know my wife?"

Teacher: What do you know about Lake Erie?
Rose: It's full of ghosts, Miss.

Woman in bed: Aaagh! Aaagh! A ghost just floated into my room!
Ghost: Don't worry, madam, I'm just passing through.

What airline do vampires travel on?
British Scareways.

What did one skeleton say to the other?
If we had any guts we'd get out of here.

Why are vampires artistic?
They're good at drawing blood.

A horrible old witch surprised all
her friends by announcing that
she was going to get married.
"But," said another old hag, "you
always said men were stupid. And
you vowed never to marry."
"Yes, I know," said the witch. "But I
finally found one who asked me."

What did the mother ghost say to
the naughty baby ghost?
Spook when you're spooken to.

What happened when Dr
Frankenstein swallowed some
uranium?
He got atomic ache.

Why did the wooden monsters
stand in a circle?
They were having a board meeting.

Dr Frankenstein decided to build an extension to his laboratory, so he crossed a cement mixer, a ghoul and a chicken. Now he's got a demon bricklayer.

What is even more invisible than the invisible ghost?
His shadow.

What's a skeleton?
Bones with the person off.

Why are Martians green?
Because they forgot to take their travel-sickness tablets.

What does Dracula say to his victims?
It's been nice gnawing you.

Why did Dracula eat strong peppermints?
Because he had bat breath.

Ghost: Do you believe in the hereafter?
Phantom: Of course I do.
Ghost: Well, hereafter leave me alone.

Did you hear about the little spook who couldn't sleep at night because his brother kept telling him human stories?

Two people went into a very dark, spooky cave. "I can't see a thing," said one.
"Hold my hand," said the other.
"All right." The first man reached out. "Take off that horrible bristly glove first, though."
"But I'm not wearing a glove . . ."

Robot: I have to dry my feet carefully after a bath.
Monster: Why?
Robot: Otherwise I get rusty nails.

What kind of ghosts haunt
hospitals?
Surgical spirits.

Did you hear about the competition to find the laziest spook in the world? All the competitors were lined up on stage. "I've got a really nice, easy job for the laziest person here," said the organizer. "Will the laziest spook raise his hand?"

All the spooks put up their hands – except one.

"Why didn't you raise your hand?" asked the presenter.

"Too much trouble," yawned the spook!

A short, fat, hairy monster was waiting for a train and decided to while away the time by weighing himself on a machine on the station platform. Once he'd weighed himself he looked at the chart that indicated the ideal weight for each height.

"Having any problems?" asked another passenger. "Are you overweight?"

"No," said the monster, "I'm just four feet too short."

Which day of the week do ghosts
like best?
Moandays.

How do phantom hens dance?
Chick to chick.

What's the best way of avoiding
infection from biting ghosts?
Don't bite any ghosts.

What do you get if you try to take a ghost's photograph?
Transparencies.

Who speaks at the ghosts' press conference?
The spooksperson.

What is a ghost's favorite dessert?
Boo-berry pie with I-scream.

Why are ghosts invisible?
They wear see-through clothes.

Why is the graveyard such a noisy place?
Because of all the coffin!

What do you get if you cross a ghost with a packet of crisps?
Snacks that go crunch in the night.

Which weight do ghosts box at?
Phantom weight.

Why did the witch put her broom in
the washing machine?
She wanted a clean sweep.

What do you call a wizard from
outer space?
A flying sorcerer.

What do you call a motor bike
belonging to a witch?
A brrooooom stick.

Why do skeletons drink milk?
Because it's good for the bones.

Why was Dracula so happy at the
races?
His horse won by a neck.

What do you get if you cross a
vampire with Al Capone?
A fangster!

How does a vampire enter his
house?
Through the bat flap.

Why are skeletons usually so calm?
Nothing gets under their skin.

How did skeletons send each other letters in the days of the Wild West?
By Bony Express.

What happens to a witch when she loses her temper?
She flies off the handle.

Why do skeletons hate winter?
Because the cold goes right through them.

How does a vampire get through
life with only one fang?
He has to grin and bare it.

If a boxer was knocked out by
Dracula, what would he be?
Out for the Count.

Why did the vampire actress turn
down so many film offers?
She was waiting for a part she
could get her teeth into.

What do you get if you cross an owl
with a vampire?
A bird that's ugly but doesn't give
a hoot.

What do you get if you cross a
vampire with a flea?
Lots of very worried dogs.